Dollars and Cents for Harriet

By Betsy and Giulio Maestro

CROWN PUBLISHERS, INC., NEW YORK

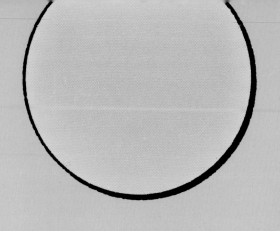

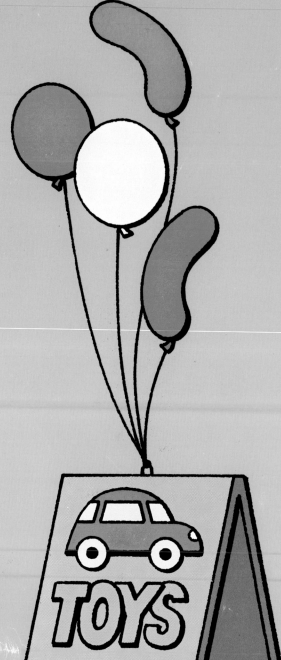

Published by Crown Publishers, Inc., 225 Park Avenue South, New York,
New York 10003 and represented in Canada by the
Canadian MANDA Group.
CROWN is a trademark of Crown Publishers, Inc.

Manufactured in Italy

Library of Congress Cataloging-in-Publication Data

Maestro, Betsy. Dollars and cents for Harriet.
Summary: As Harriet attempts to earn five dollars for a new kite, the
reader learns about coins that add up to a dollar.
1. Money – United States – Juvenile literature.
[1. Money] I. Maestro, Giulio. II. Title.
HG221.5.M24 1988   332.4'973   88-287

ISBN 0-517-56958-2

10 9 8 7 6 5 4 3 2 1

First Edition

Harriet looked into the store window.
She saw just what she wanted.
It cost five dollars.

At home, she emptied all the pennies from her bank. Harriet had learned that one hundred pennies make one dollar. "I'll count them," said Harriet.

Each penny is one cent, so Harriet counted by ones. "1, 2, 3, 4, 5, 6, . . ." By the time she reached ". . . 98, 99, 100," she was out of breath. "100 cents! I do have a dollar!" she said.

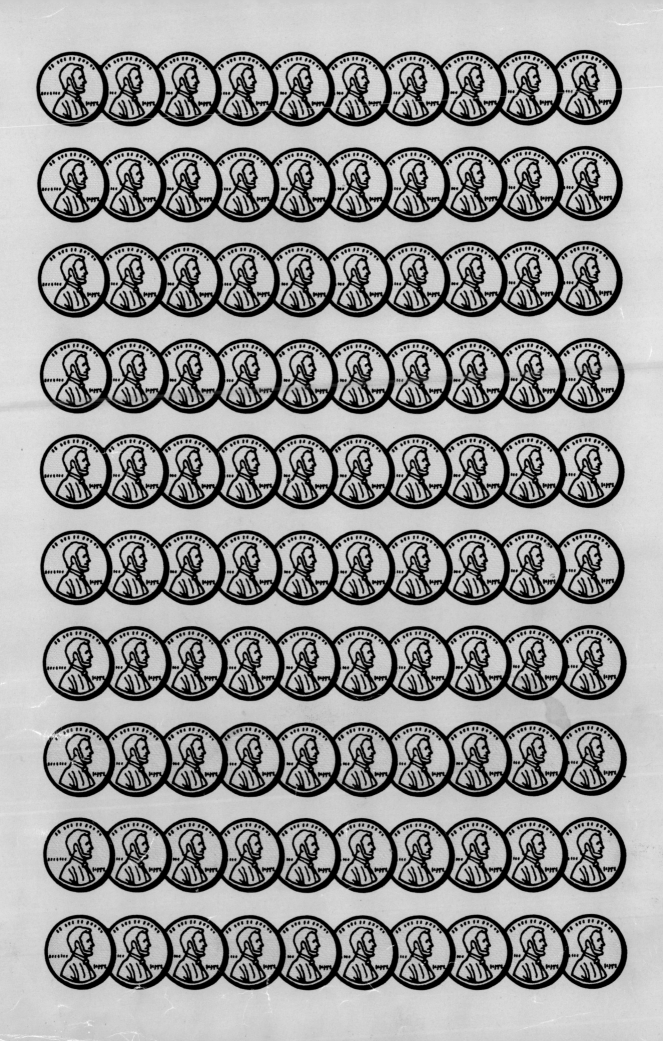

She still needed four more dollars.
Harriet thought about ways to earn
some money.

At Snake's house, Harriet got a job mowing the lawn. "Thanks," said Snake as he paid Harriet. Harriet took home a lot of nickels.

Harriet knew that each nickel is five cents, so she counted the nickels by fives. "5, 10, 15, 20, 25, 30, 35, 40, 45, 50, 55, 60, 65, 70, 75, 80, 85, 90, 95, 100. 100 cents! Another dollar! Now I have two dollars."

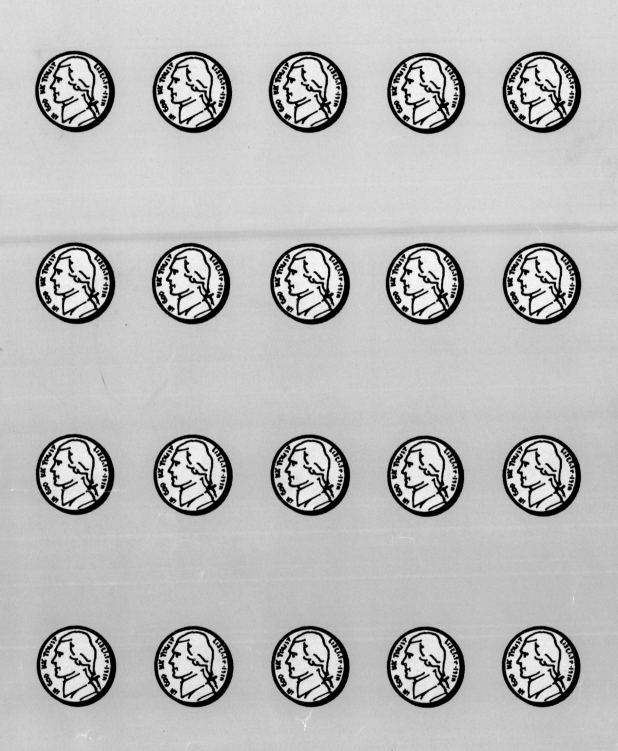

Harriet still needed three more dollars.
At Cat's house, Harriet weeded the
garden. "Here you are, Harriet," said
Cat as she paid her for the work.
Harriet went home with a handful
of dimes.

Each dime is ten cents, so Harriet counted the dimes by tens. "10, 20, 30, 40, 50, 60, 70, 80, 90, 100. 100 cents! Another dollar!" shouted Harriet. "Now I have three dollars!"

Harriet only needed two more dollars. At Giraffe's house, she swept the porch and steps. "You did a great job," said Giraffe. She gave Harriet some quarters for her work.

Counting the four quarters was easy. "25, 50, 75, 100. 100 cents! Another dollar!" Now Harriet had four dollars. She only needed one more.

At Monkey's house, Harriet saw a very dirty car. She washed it. "You made it shine. Thanks, Harriet," said Monkey as he handed her two half-dollars.

Harriet knew she had another dollar.
Each half-dollar is fifty cents,
so two half-dollars make one whole dollar.
"50 cents and 50 cents are 100 cents,"
said Harriet. "Now I have the five dollars!"

Harriet put her hundred pennies, her twenty nickels, her ten dimes, her four quarters, and her two half-dollars into a bag. The five dollars were very heavy. At the bank, she traded her five dollars in coins for five crisp, new dollar bills. They were easy to carry.

At the store, Harriet gave her five
dollar bills to Ostrich at the counter.
Ostrich gave her a big package.
"Have fun," she said.

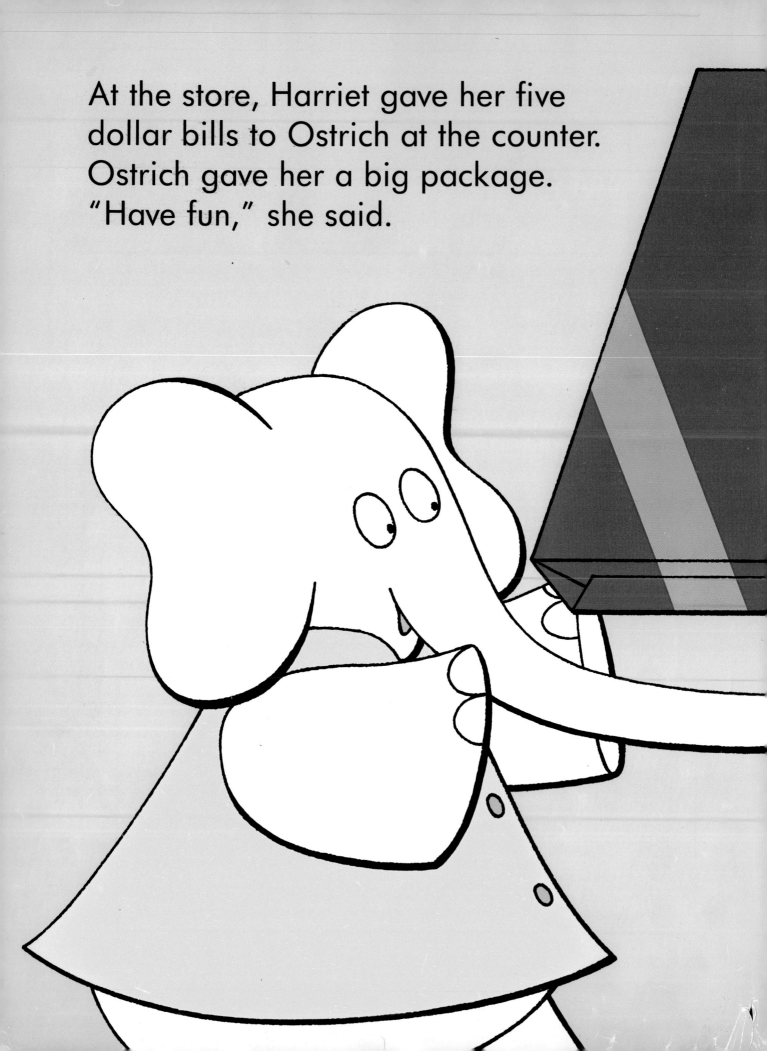

Harriet carried her big package to the park. The wind was blowing. It was a perfect day for flying her new kite!

DATE DUE		
JAN 5 1999		
MAR 1 4 1999		
MAR 2 5 1999		
SEP 1 4 1999		
OCT 5 1999		
FEB 8 2000		
MAR 0 1 2000		
MAR 2 8 2000		
AUG 2 2000		